SYCAMORE

SYCAMORE

poems

KATHY FAGAN

MILKWEED EDITIONS

Published 2017 by Milkweed Editions
Printed in the United States of America
Cover design by Michael Kellner
Cover art by Yang Xinguang, *There Are Stones Below Iron* (2011; wire, plywood, stone; 120 x 120 x
55 cm)
Author photo by Fritha Strand
19 20 21 22 23 6 5 4 3 2
First Edition

Milkweed Editions, an independent nonprofit publisher, gratefully acknowledges sustaining support
from the Jerome Foundation; the Lindquist & Vennum Foundation; the McKnight Foundation;
the National Endowment for the Arts; the Target Foundation; and other generous contributions from
foundations, corporations, and individuals. Also, this activity is made possible by the voters of
Minnesota through a Minnesota State Arts Board Operating Support grant, thanks to a legislative
appropriation from the arts and cultural heritage fund, and a grant from the Wells Fargo Foundation.
For a full listing of Milkweed Editions supporters, please visit milkweed.org.

Library of Congress Cataloging-in-Publication Data

Fagan, Kathy, author.
Sycamore : poems / Kathy Fagan.
First edition. | Minneapolis, Minnesota : Milkweed Editions, 2017.
        p. cm.
LCCN 2016041134 | ISBN 9781571314734 (paperback)
BISAC: POETRY / American / General.
LCC PS3556.A326 A6 2017
DDC 811/.54—dc23
LC record available at https://lccn.loc.gov/2016041134

CONTENTS

Once in a sycamore I was glad
all at the top, and I sang.

Then came a departure.

—JOHN BERRYMAN

PLATANACEAE FAMILY TREE

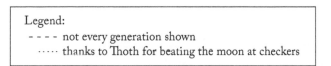

Legend:
- - - - not every generation shown
····· thanks to Thoth for beating the moon at checkers

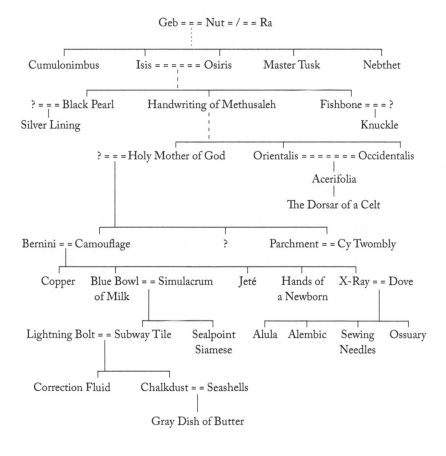

Geb = = = Nut = / = = Ra

Cumulonimbus   Isis = = = = = = Osiris   Master Tusk   Nebthet

? = = = Black Pearl   Handwriting of Methusaleh   Fishbone = = = ?
Silver Lining   Knuckle

? = = = Holy Mother of God   Orientalis = = = = = = = Occidentalis

Acerifolia

The Dorsar of a Celt

Bernini = = Camouflage   ?   Parchment = = Cy Twombly

Copper   Blue Bowl = = Simulacrum   Jeté   Hands of   X-Ray = = Dove
of Milk   a Newborn

Lightning Bolt = = Subway Tile   Sealpoint   Alula   Alembic   Sewing   Ossuary
Siamese   Needles

Correction Fluid   Chalkdust = = Seashells

Gray Dish of Butter

I

CARO NOME

Jets shake the air and snow
breaks off a tree branch in little puffs. One
cardinal. Cars moving slowly downhill on the ice.

It is always someone's last day.
Dearest Bird, she read from the card she'd found unattached to the flowers,
Happy Day To Our Sweetest Hart. Love Monster And Beef Dad.

Their secret language.
Manischewitz, she calls me for the sweetness.
Manitoba, for the expanse.

Deer rest in snow,
charcoal muzzle to charcoal hoof, heads slung over
their shoulders like swans.

One is in REM. Look at it dreaming, she said.
Fern buttons unwheel in a dark place behind the snow,
a contrast she loves in me.

The sledding hill is closed, the days like an unused billboard,
but sunsets have been fantastic,
jewel-toned as the flowers unattached to the card, or hot like the cardinal

who pins the whole picture up
with your eye. Meanwhile,
her tree is an iron room with the moon inside. Its branches

have a mental disorder so sunsets keep dodging them.
I am the color of that tree
she loves and nearly as still. And my blood, which is not in this picture,

will soon cool, sunset winking out in my eyes and her eyes
welling in a language that once fell and rose
in drifts then melted, starry, she said, starry, into my warm coat.

CINDER

after "Disquieting Landscapes," demolition video by Cyprien Gaillard

I'm worried about the house and its snotty new crybaby face.
Something under the siding froze in the blizzard then followed the icicles
down but only partway. What's under my skin is
opposite, like cinder, burning but barely, nearly extinguished.
It fell from the El like snow sometimes I'd want to catch it on my tongue.
It's worse at night when something smells not quite like home but ashen
and tremors move inside my thighs as if I'd ridden my bike to a moon
I shouldn't have. Her voice is not her T-shirt though it can feel like her
heat on my ribs if I want it to. When I close my eyes I see
the exhibit's demolition loop: roving spot, fireworks, the crowd
a safe distance away. Built in 1958 in the suburbs of Paris,
the building is nondescript: 51 years × 40 units × an average of 2.2 inhabitants
per unit per year for an average of 16 years apiece = what?
No one wants to do the math anymore unless there's dynamite involved.
But where do they go, mouths shaped in little Os of expectation?
Is that how they recognize each other at the current and the singe?
When the building collapses toward its center, like Topsy the famous
electrocuted elephant, not even the dust stays airborne long.

SNOW GLOBE

after *Encounters at the End of the World* by Werner Herzog

With booms & chirrs seals
speak under the ice of an ocean
frozen over.
Stationary ocean. Electrified song.
Color: snow day with autumn
leaves inside it,
glassine sheers of cantaloupe & kiwi on
lavender, gunmetal, jetwing—
                    When you rode the elephant through
the puncture, the first syllable of my name
parted the deep with your beautiful hand.
Sparrow shuddered in her dustbath, swath of pleasure
raked up
        & out.
                This is where I sat
in the avalanche.
                In winter,
where I was born,
you pulled a cord of silk in your beautiful hand.
I heard nothing
under the ice. *Bye-bye now,* our people would say.
Bye-bye later.
First, song,
            a detonation—
then white everywhere.

SYCAMORES AT HIGH NOON

Chalk on the blackboard
dry, I'm chalk on the street. I'm I I I.
I am your outline, your line out,
your line up, your lesson,
Kilimanjaros infinitum,
choirs of whitewashed
roller coasters past.
Gully, you know me:
the silver linings, apostolic, lab-coated
host of me. Advancing like a wood,
more ghostly than Banquo,
I cast no shadow.
And vertically I barely creak
in wind that raised and hung me
out to dry, broken in several places,
breaking all the day I need.

POEM WITH ITS HEART BURIED UNDER THE FLOORBOARDS

You have been frowning a long time now, Mr. Poe.
For a long time grandfathers & their charges have been
walking from the library into days of black & white.
Large cars move funereally under black trees, black
birds; the sky is white, the lawns white where snow
has fallen. In spite of the snow, nothing is beautiful,
& it is always 4 o'clock on a Sunday, post meridiem.
The floor may creak—a *cri de coeur*—
but outside two teens outpace a white panel truck
climbing uphill in the slush. For a long time
the wheels have been spinning, Mr. Poe.
Our charges do not hear. Nor do they speak,
their earbuds white as snow.
They have some place to get to & they go.

THE WHITE, THE RED & THE PINK IN-BETWEEN

When the wall I say I've hit gives
under my hand like skin I'm told
Breathe deeply

but if I did my ribs would crack like a book
like the nave's ceiling with its grayed teeth grinding
away on the old story
                              She must be
in the pages somewhere
in the drifting snow of February

She must be

                              here
in the petals held aloft like planets & suddenly
soft as bathwater on the back of my hand

in the cottonwood flurry & catalpa trash of May

&   like film catching fire
                              here
at last
in the hemorrhage of summer roses
                              the canopy of crisp
blood & Cro-Magnon brow of the Japanese maple

She must be here
                              somewhere
within the gothic bones of my rib cage
riding the twin gales Sorrow & Desire

queen of the rodeo

Once I held her to me

                                        I held her

long &
in me

our skin breath bones blood one

                              story

chewed off like a limb

CONVENT OF SANTA CHIARA AND THE POOR CLARES

San Damiano, Assisi

Through the Porta Nuova,
past olive groves and cypress
on the way to San Damiano,

is the tiny chapel of San Feliciano,
size of a vault and locked
like one, a stone-encrusted

Fabergé egg. A gilded Madonna
panel glows inside via
no discernible source of light.

Downhill, the convent of the Poor
Clares is also filled with light,
though the rooms are small,

the walls thick, the vistas glaringly
vast. Here, on her stone
pillow, one can imagine

the moon. Santa Chiara.
San Francesco. She dressed
his stigmatic hands in chamois.

She sewed for him his robes.
Hours ago, my lover's hands
moved inside me for the last time.

Birds swam in the circles
of the matin bells. There were
so many times. There were

so many stones, not one
with a memory of the hand
that laid it or a thought

for the bells that play day
and night, dust rising, resettling.
My hair, once gold

leaf aloft in the wind, fades
like day from the hills.
If I look cold, lay bells over

me, the moon. If I look pale,
come closer: my light is
inside where she left it.

KABOOM PANTOUM

I'll ring the bells,
Ohio, tomorrow,
when stars come due
like lice to a grackle.

Ohio, tomorrow
is winter & every winter,
like lice on a grackle,
we must drive defensively.

This winter & every winter,
I wait too long to wear a coat.
We must dress defensively,
but last minute still counts.

If I wait to wear a coat,
will you wait with me?
Last minutes still count,
maybe more than last words.

Will you wait with me?
Take *sequoia*, for example—
maybe more than last words
word games reveal a lot—

sequoia, for example, is
the shortest word to use each vowel once.
Word games reveal a lot.
Short word. Tall tree. AEIOU.

The tallest tree to use each vowel once
does not thrive in Ohio.
Short word. *I*. Double *O*. No UAE.
Bell in the mouth at either end.

.

THE PLANE TREES OF THE SEINE

stone bruised & empty   like pansies
        in my heart   & thin-legged
like them my arms   have teeth
        my mouth   barbed bridges
cathedrals that we are   & there are
locks on the bridges   of love & of travel
& though I have   the raccoon eyes
for it & convex   belly I will not
        starve   behind their bars
nor will I rattle   tornadically
no from my   snow there emerges
        an   unmonumental
something
                unbeloved   unbereft

SYCAMORE STACKED IN LENGTHS & PIECES

Statuary, take away air, equals odalisque,
All oracular torso and mottled ass in shades of blush and butter
Cream, unspooling drapery of pachyderm gray.

Not ossuary exactly, for while I rest I do not rest
In peace, grounded dirigible in mid-deflate, and newly tritanopic, too,
My blues gone brown and lichen-scaled.

Massive as Constantine's knees, I am dumb runes,
I am quarry, querulous. More stone than wood, I will not burn.
More flesh than stone, I will not carve.

Dropped from air, born of water, I hold
The water. It is all I hold.

O witching wand, do not wish me well when you find me—
Or the slag of the one-story, low-ceilinged self that passes for me now.
As you pass, though I look impassive, pass over.

SYCAMORE IN THE WEAK LIGHT OF EARLY SPRING

Pettable as brushed
     nickel or skim
milk, newly
     sprouted silver
pubes and snowdrops
     suddenly dotting
the duff, the weak
     light of early spring
blows forth a self-
     portrait with no self
in it. Freshets
     rush under
curbside ice crusts—
     everything runs down
the gutter lanes.
     The old pelt,
bleached with lice
     and weather, goes
too—only the finite
     today springing forward.

SANTA CATERINA'S TOMB

Santa Maria sopra Minerva, Rome

On her feast day, recumbent under
glass, Saint Catherine was open
for business. We queued up to touch her
hand, that never learned to write,

a hand original
to her body, most of which rests
here, waxy fallen pillar
in a church built over
a temple, virgin on goddess.

Catherine's head lies at home
in Siena. Her heart could be
in my breast pocket right now—
something's dead in there.

Touching her reminded me of the match
stick we used for the votives;

of fava shells we piled together at table;
of our lips out of practice;
of the lily, her emblem;
and of the sycamore, which is mine.

Having painted the miracle of blood
sacrifice again and again, word

made flesh, angel
wings of gold and mica, Fra Angelico
rests nearby.
                So you lay
beside me once, my body so often
a ruin beneath you.

SYCAMORE, WICK & FLAME

With my wet feet
and thinning hair,
with what passes for river
and what passes as weather,
with my dark patches
and bright spots, I'm
camouflage, a shrugger,
reflecting nothing, a molting
wolf, all upward
expansion, not a thought
for my roots.

                    4:17
is my digital time. Akimbo,
the spoken word.
When I'm found by a hand
in a series of hands,
I pool like milk in a blue bowl.
There's a key out there
lying in the grass,
and then there's me,
not looking for it.

II

LETTER TO WHAT'S MOSTLY MISSING

after Christopher Howell's "He Writes to the Soul"

At first I thought I'd write
you about the sycamore that won't dress for supper,
preferring its white limbs bare, and how the oak
it dotes on returns the favor by offering chartreuse
hankies on every hand. Then I thought that's just me
again, swapping summer for supper, canopy for canapé,
and surely we're beyond that now. So instead I guess
I'll give you news of the silver lining, which was dreaming
until Wednesday when it woke to say Cloud, Sun,
Sliver of Glass. Lucky for me I was wearing my safety
goggles and asbestos gloves at the time. Lucky the pink
heat had my hair to burn or who knows what limestone
brimstone Joan of Arc shit I'd be subjected to next.
It was the meteorological opposite of that time
in the graveyard cracking ice with my boot heels
off the headstones to find her. All that pristine weather
and footwear later to discover: dead is still dead.
That's what our ghost says anyway. She says
she hears us best when we can't speak. She's
nicknamed you Kodak—for the colorful memories
we create, I suppose—or perhaps it was Kodiak she said
through the ice. In any case, one can only ask how many
names for the past there are. I am one. You may be
more like the alarm clock sounding off out of nowhere,
and the boy sprinting toward it and me on his way,
who met me as warmly as if he were mine. I think,
for a moment, he thought that, too. When we refer to
parallel lives, don't we mean lives lived besides?

That's all for now, except to say that, unlike other trees,
the sycamore's bark can't expand, so it just breaks off,
which accounts for its Bernini-like sheen. The old ones
are nearly hollow, therefore unstable. The fox and rabbit
like to make their dens inside. Empty isn't always
the opposite of perfectly full. The oak says, Let me spread
this mantle of blue over your cold marble shoulders,
Sycamore. And what can she say but yes.

SHOO FLY

Scratch the ponderosa pine & you get
butterscotch. What she meant was nick it.
She used her hatchet.
Amber ensued. A pudding.
She snapped the cape to her Subaru & flew it.
Say you were bad at rations & the scent faded.
Say it was hopscotch she'd meant all along.
That season was diamond-hard & you the occlusion in it.
The next was a Flemish painting & you the pit in the stone fruit.
Pain is a quarantine all its own.
It comes with padded earphones & a joystick.
Hear the tone close hear the tone farther.
Stars explode in the head & you squeeze squeeze squeeze.
Say you were bad at weather & the chalk faded.
Say it was another tune you'd wanted all along.
Suddenly you're eating soft-serve on a ferry & singing
campfire songs under Orion.
Here are the willows skip to my lou.
Here are the roses skip to my lou.
She skipped it my darling my darling now you.

ELELENDISH

The palazzo di Maia flushed coral at dusk,
blossom of rosy chocolate, bowl of oxblood bloom.

When dusk falls in Godthåb, now known as Nuuk,
reindeer lick the fawns clean, eat placenta off snow,

the tundra spotted with birth each May, with spring
lichen and low, red cabins, like flowering quince

at our latitudes. Ancient herders honored the ox,
crowned it leader of a new alphabet. In another story,

because its sound is silent, God rewarded the humble
letter with first place. Only one in three reindeer

bears a live calf anymore, but warm as the earth gets,
no one will ever instruct an Inuit to cut flowers

on a slant with a sharp knife in the cool part of day.
Quince will never bloom there, or set its fruit,

which is a pome, and in its raw state inedible,
but once bletted, makes a sweet liqueur or marmalade.

COTTONWOOD

The cottonwood pollen is flying again,
Adrift like snow or ash. It lines
The curbs, it sticks to my lips
Like down to a fox's muzzle.
I made a poem about it years ago.
We were new then. We'd set fire
To our old lives and made love day
And night, mouths full of each other.
Back then, we were a match
For June: arrogant, promising, feverish.
For as long as we live, summer returns
To us. And snow, ash, they, too, return.

HEADS

After we broke
        up we went
                shopping for hats.

In those days
        there were a vast
                number of hats,

few of them
        flattering. After
                I dropped you

at Departures, I found
        the words *square*
                haloes of the

living. I am
        a safe and efficient
                driver. In under

twenty minutes I can
        spot three or four
                places I could

live or may already be
        living in. More
                inclination than

skill, it's as if
    someday I will
        make the next

right, turn
    left at the light,
        and bring the groceries in

to Apartment 5.
    Your face is too
        small for most hats.

My face is too
    big for my hair.
        The square haloes fit

us like picture frames
    we eventually place face-
        down in your head or mine.

SYCAMORE ENVIES THE COTTONWOODS BEHIND YOUR PLACE

You're high gloss and order in the newest streetlamps,
All your little birdies come home to roost.

Does every blessed species kick off in its sleep
The covers, the leaves, the loam, and the leagues?

He, she, and it pass, the one altricial need;
At their lips is pressed the ribbon I'm meant to twist

Into ornament: remember me, my streaming
Seed, night and its coat-tailing meteors . . .

So once went my habit of mind: poppies, paper, stars.
Tonight the tenderer planets take cover,

Bodies abuzz in their own demise.

NO METEOR

The night one
      gold star shook
loose from blue
      firmament, I learned
they were neither
      star nor blue. Just space
junk in sky I only
      perceived as blue.
I was right
      they could kill me,
junk and atmosphere,
      wrong that either
tried, neither an over-
      achiever. More the tired
kind, the kind I tend to
      adore, that I perceive
might write *adore*
      in light I see as fire, or,
soon enough, as ice.
      Adore is Latin,
to entreat. *Meteor*,
      Greek for lofty. How
the lofty have fallen,
      up or down, depends
entirely on one's point
      of view. But when you
said, *I adore you*, what
      I heard was
the entreaty to entreat,
      and adored you back.

I fell from there to here
          with the velocity
of a fat, hot tear.
          I'm no meteor,
so I looked it up:
          how long it takes
a meteor to fall.
          Related searches:
how long it takes to fall
          in love/how long
it takes to fall
          out of love/how long
it takes to fall
          asleep. One might think
no time at all.

DIAGNOSIS

I wasn't made to live alone. One
night there's a sky with clouds by Magritte,
the next I'm headed over the guardrail,
and who do I tell? My Ideal Reader?
Choices narrow as we age,
like my spine in the nave of its body.
I grew hollow waiting for your face,
like a drum beneath a hand that never
opens. To say *sail* is too nautical,
to say *soufflé*—well, then I forget
what I'm talking about . . .
          The ocean stayed still.
And the cows stayed still on the hills
between us.
          I don't know if my spine will
ever close its trefoil window. I don't know
if I will never see you again. It is inferred
or it is infrared. Either way, my leaves fell.
And it took a good while, but I grew new
ones. Then the birds came back.

BLACK WALNUTS

                    Their cases fall,
Split & whole, in the cemetery grass,
With no one to see them. Sulphuric green
& Naugahyde, the fruit rock-hard inside,
They stink out loud, with no one to smell them.

It is the season of separation & falling
Away. Sycamore bark tears off in sheets,
But I won't be writing on them—
They prefer to roll,
Empty, on either side of the river.

The river is less like a horse or time than I am,
A fissure that fills & empties without comment.
It may flirt with the weather, turn pretty or brooding
Under a gaze, but it splits east & west just the same,
Keeping each for itself. It never feels

Frivolous, selfish, or deadly. It doesn't fear
Bridges. It's got its banks, its silt, its delta,
Its nuts, its bark, its currents, its tenants,
Its playlists, the occasional flip of its hair.
All that & more, while no one is looking.

July & August, downhill with no hands.
A magician shut in her dark box:
Gone before the key can find the lock.

STRIDE

Mediterranean teal
crosses the lap
pool in German

rectangles of Ohio
sun. Up above,
my stride on

the treadmill is far
too long—Michael's
moonwalk, fan

full in my face.
I can walk West
Side Story, too,

but mostly like
orphaned animals
from Disney. Those

I meet here—
the overdressed seniors,
kids trembling

on their way
to the waterslide,
the beauties and bulkers—

have so many skins,
so many musics
playing in their ears.

Every day I choose
Quick Start,
All Terrain,

but somehow I always
end up on the hill
to the church with you:

stone, wax,
the rosewood
saints, crypts

underfoot, fonts
at our elbows, the jangling
coins of infinite intention—

and in the frescoed
distance, real and pictured,
sun, stone pine, poplar.

In that Old World,
I walk smiling
into the jaws

of lions, certain
I will
not be harmed.

STRUCTURAL ENGINEERING

The juvenile giraffe was shot and butchered
Before onlookers. We had risen from our moat of fucking
To view the footage. Zookeepers feeding its shoulder
To the lions. It was the most beautiful piece of meat
We had ever seen. Out of context
The pattern of its coat seemed even more
Desirable, explaining apparel and home
Décor. We had risen from our moat to give
The child the toy giraffe. She named it
Pisa. Patterns so powerful they can't fight back.
Like this building my metaphorical heart lives on in.
Tall ruin sheltering no one. But look
How it frames the infinite. Nature
Ravishing my every inch.

ODE TO JULIA MORGAN

1872–1957, the first woman licensed to practice architecture in California

The trochees of our names have drawn
rectangles below
the blue vaults of the swimming pool.
Rich men. Poor men.
So many animals in the zoo.
An elephant stands at the edge of a ditch
where another has fallen and died.
Do animals grieve? the scientists ask.
Look at her eyes.
Egyptians called themselves Cattle of the Sun
God, born as they were of his tears and sweat.
Limestone cutaways in West Virginia
weep each winter. The face of the whole
planet's a wailing wall
and scientists ask, Do they grieve?

Even here, Julia Morgan, bougainvillea cascading,
the On/Off of whitecaps,
white lines of the freeway,
cows on the hillsides (live stock),
and stars like a landscape in a landscape of gravity holding it
all. There are so many

plans, Julia Morgan. So many extant, destroyed, and repurposed
dwellings. In one, the scientists ask
their question. In another, you are dying alone.
Which one is blown by spring
winds across the tarmac, its own feathers working

against it? Which one have I not yet been?
I, He, She, and It grieve. Why do they
ask? California. West Virginia. Mountains
making fuel and mountains making beaches. We are each
our own industry, the cow and its god.
Draw me a lotus
flower, Julia Morgan, a pool
like a chapel.
A room like a poem.
Our names are drawn on our graves already.

LIFE, WITH EYELINER

after *And the Ships Sails On* by Federico Fellini

Fellini's ship sunk in undulant lamé. The soprano sung an aria through it, and later wore it to the wrap party. Nor did the refugees drown, but emigrated and multiplied, bequeathing nothing to their children but their wiles and animal magnetism.

The rat lying drowned at the curb near the storm drain is not a rat but a dead puppy. Is one duty of art, likewise, to turn revulsion to sympathy?

When the Gulf receded, Katrina survivors widely tattooed themselves with fleurs de lis, an emblem of New Orleans. Hospitalized for hepatitis, one citizen said, I like my tattoos like my disasters: homemade.

French monarchs adopted fleurs de lis from the Florentine Medicis; its upright stem, standards, and falls, like a sword or a cross in a field. Some see penises, uncircumcised.

The Capuchins of Rome arranged the bones of their dead to resemble French scrolls and rosettes. The original Corvette bore the fleur de lis logo as a nod to the heritage of Louis Chevrolet; Detroit displays it on its flag.

The eye Fellini cast on life, on death, was less cold than kohled: grotesque but sweet. When the water rises, working men and women know to park their Chevys aimed uphill, for all the good it does them, gassed to the golden hilt.

SYCAMORE IN JERICHO

Year 33 of Agnus Dei,
Zac the taxman shimmies up to better see
the Christ Parade: Parable Mirabilis, Parabola Miraculous.
I knew the stories: the blind sighted,
the dead alive, the cult of boys all
soon-to-be-snoring at the soon-gored side.

So I say: Little man,
it is easier for a hundred needles to dance
on the head of an angel than for a camel to enter
the kingdom of God on the back
of a tiny tax collector.

Jesus, Sycamore, he said,
without exasperation.

And then the Christ looked up and said,
Come down from there, Zacchaeus, and he did.
And after, I felt, for a long time after, a weight on me then,
a heated impression, hotter than the sun's,
like a word can leave or the memory of a child
in one's arms.

So when the people pointed after them, snarling
about sin, I understood
their fear, which was feeling:
how it burns.

RUIN

I couldn't say the year for certain.
Two millennia and a Judas tree at least.
Time passing, like most of it,
without me or the wife, poor wide apples,
scraped off a board with the back of a knife.

I heard *Title Divine is Mine*
even when the house don't stand.
I heard *Wait to Go, Borrowed Tine,*
Flexible Flame, and your name, your name.

I could feel the money running down my back,
like that popper we pulled confetti out of.
My thoughts litter
like that: Honey, keep racing. Honey, hold on,
you are out on a limb—

And then, because our bodies were the tree,
it said, Ouch, ouch, ouch.
It said, OK, tornado,
do what you can do,
rain down your version of things.

Thanks to its amnestic effect,
the versed administered won't let us remember
how hard we are trying to forget—
e.g., the key I

taped to the plague with your name on it,
to your locker, the plaque, the wreath, the lager,
a luster of yellow lanterns reflected on the lacquer
of the blacker Lethe canal.

HOW WE LOOKED

       didn't matter for once
because we were flying.

       The crows we were
clothed in took a running

       start for the gothic
and that was all:

       tooled doors opened
and waxy air

       lifted us on its current.
And though the jeweled

       light was dim we could tell
the faces we were

       seeing were beautiful,
each with a mouth

       and voice, and there was
no doubt then,

       as our chins and our rib cages,
our wrists and our knees

       rose, that what mattered
was that we obey

       for once, and when
the voices said,

       Look up, Look up,
though rain fell

in our eyes, we did.

III

THE SIGNAL MASTER'S SONG

I read *Exeunt* aloud from the reality play & it heard me
I carried its bags out
I packed its car
It could have shipped to Europe that way & never shifted its contents
A grove of sycamores stood by like wilis
I invited the Arctic in
I asked the snow with its rose horizon to lie down beside me & let me weep in its arms
I was like Paris all piano
I was the bulb that wouldn't force
I consulted maps drew my own asked for directions took copious notes
I lowered my gaze in the manner of the Virgin
Cimabue Leonardo mild-mannered barely smiling
I had the feeling it took a long time to get here & always had
I believed the world was done with metaphor & then the leaves came into bud
I mistook sunrise for sunset & I corrected my mistake
I made many more mistakes & corrected almost all of them
        except for the ones that would become the best stories
I thought my heart would break into pieces until I heard my neighbor's cat
He said *stationary ocean, baby everything, marshy hope*
He favored adjective-noun combinations no matter how strongly I objected
I invited summer in with its freak hailstones the size & color of human teeth
We ate ox together
It lingered like an odor of sugar in the cabin
I had in short my wings de-iced
And the flag became the country then
And I rose through the shortest light waves
Pink agapanthus on a tall blue stem

SUBURBAN CANTICLE

With your beard full of mice and a mouth full of hymns you sang for them.
Wearing offal perfume, all five wounds seeping and your blind eyes tearing
    in the sun, Francesco, you sang.
Iconic now, you are everyone's neighbor, spotted with birdlime among
    the mounds of daylilies that crack out
    their embers in the middle of June.

Crayolas crushed on the sidewalk are named Caribbean Turquoise and Sunflower Gold;
I didn't have to read their paper wrappers to know this.
I didn't toss in the dryer sheet or lay down the mulch around here either,
    but these are our top and our bottom notes now.

The Global Fellowship of Future Saints runs in soccer socks on Razor scooters.
Fireflies light the night for you, saith the Lord, and you shall have dominion
over all the creatures you spy with your little eye as you lie
    on your back watching clouds float by.

We're alike, Francesco.
I, too, was a child among gas mowers, picking warm tar from my foot soles.
The blades of the rotary fan reflected my days like a flip-book.
I was devout for such a long time, but wore my summer clothes and walked
    barefoot on the bees and their clover so briefly.

Because you reside beside them in heaven,
you know that Anne Sexton pastes firecrackers into her scrapbook
and Joseph Cornell hoards fan magazines.
That's like us, too, Francesco:
    metaphorical yet concrete.

Let me be clear:

   If I pray to you on my knees under the sycamore, I am asking you to let us stay.
Like the honeysuckle, we love it here. We don't care who we crowd out.

WAITING AREA ATRIUM

The grapes we fed the baby kept her occupied and smiling, and let us talk the way
adults do under pressure, with food and forced good humor. But when we discovered
the grapes had seeds, our palms flew instantly to her chin, our pleading voices kicked
in: Spit it out. Spit it out. Did you swallow? Swallow? Swallow? She had. Then
swallowed again, mutely, to prove her point. The silhouettes of swallows kept real birds
from crashing into the windows of the atrium, where I'd been directed after leaving
my lover in pre-op. Who knew where we'd be after? I was to wait in the Waiting Area
Atrium while they took off her breasts. The windows were too tall to see through,
but surrounded us on all sides. East and west allowed light in above mountain ranges
laser-etched into the glass; I thought of them as the Appalachians and the Rockies.
North and south were dark, like the poles. I'd come from some direction and could
now wait here, as if I had traveled a great distance, over both sets of frosted mountains,
the pack mule I'd long suspected I was, picking a path through the valley. One hears
the phrase, Can't put one foot in front of the other, but never expects to feel it. Can't or
won't, my parents would ask, but what was the answer? Your baby girl ate the grapes.
She swallowed the seeds; she didn't choke. A year from now her brothers will be born
behind the windows of the North Pole. The scars on my lover's chest, two seams in a
quarry. But we don't know any of that yet. We tear the grapes to pulp before we eat
them, though they'd tasted good as they were: small, hard, cool, the seeds sliding down
our throats or cracking under our teeth. What had we been so afraid of, hands covered
with juice, seeds piled on our plate? The world was already rising around us; all we had
to do was wait.

SPLIT

And then, on the thinnest day, I wrapped our shadows
Around me for warmth, the tail-end of orioles like embers
And the ashes they become, nectar left bubbling in a bottle
A reminder of all I never saw coming coming true: field stubble
Alive with rabbits, and the dark above our bed made one breath
And two wings darker by the bat that entered under the window sash:

> What dreams did it hear to find us,
> To what hunt was it drawn, to what murmurs, like prey?

> Old love, I forget faster and faster—
> You always parted my legs with your hand—

And still I understand
Almost nothing.

MIDDLE-AGED SYCAMORE

How frosty you are in middle age,
Sycamore, just as you were in youth,
only more grateful, if weary of the gratitude
it takes to feel alive.
By the time you light your noontime pipe,
tweens are waking up to J-pop
and widows aim their Lincoln Towncars home.
The rest of us keep waiting for the end of the world
because we're pretty sure fried foods are involved.
From Ticonderoga to far Tortuga we're aching
to know who thinks they can dance,
who's married in Grant's Tomb,
what bread tastes best with beets and Boursin cheese,
while your claque parses Mahler in the armory-turned
museum built 12½ degrees off-grid.
A crooked fortress is thine
art. I see that in you.
I see in you the poppies swaying through the wreckage,
milites gloriosi kicking dust storms down your road.
If captured, say you went to the Kroger
to buy sugar for the hummingbirds.
I confess we often thought of you as twee.
Later, when I saw a mason drilling bricks out of a church,
you became to me a Jude considerably less obscure,
like when the Rose of Sharon drops
its blossoms in the street like used tampons.
Sorry to be crude. I've seen the way you look
among a family whose limbs
make a circuitry of white nerves,
a pattern of pleading invitations like a child's *WATCH ME*s.

I, too, like the deep
green of leaves in rain and the birds
inside them. That was our mistake:
thinking what we care for
should care for us. We all want to be loved
as bees love the balm, but we should know by now
that *is* how we were loved. For one moment,
ravished, adored, unrecognizable
even to ourselves,
except for the jeté something inside us made when no one was looking.
It smelled like maple syrup and stayed still as a statue.
That's how I can tell
you only look cool to the touch.

TO YOU FOR WHOM I BROKE

one promise,
I will not break
another.

The snow deals
prepositions:
on, around, through.

It makes me want to stop
breathing.
A snowflake's singularity

becomes the burdensome
accumulation.
Creatures cocoon

in comas of survival.
I survived by falling
with it, I burned and blew,

never slept.
I walked and walked and walked
until

the meat of me
shone in glossy parcels,
like that buck we bought,

ice-hard, heavy,
remarkably clean. It pitched
an arctic station

in our freezer. We would never
eat it all,
though there were

often, there were
many times
the snow

led with conjunctions.
Sycamores let it
get on their nerves.

We watched
their breakdown
in the sky,

till all was white
on white on white.
I'll never write

a poem to you again.
You know that is a promise
I can keep.

I leave it
to the snow to
and and and and and—

NERVURE

Yes, of course there is a face in the sky, hair aglow and afloat,
an unforgettable face set not so squarely in our sites every time
a lid gets opened. As a child I believed Pandora to be
the ballerina in my jewelry box, that grace and evil arrived
spring-loaded. But O, to be loaded in winter! Cheeks packed
with mackerel and martinis, February merely a nightmare
from which we awaken ten pounds thinner, our coats
intact. Ogives of sleep have pressed into our thighs, buds
are blinding on the yew, and pop-up thaws flow a loud celadon
children can drink from. Squirrels drag their trains like runaway
brides. Mantic births follow. Deer drop to their knees, fawns
scrambling into their own white spots. They bleat like sheep,
activating, wherever they step, Dark Matter's automatic doors,
appearing and disappearing at will. On the other hand, I am
tortured by the physics of everyday life. While slicing bread
on the diagonal, I can never remember if the alien cycles
toward the past or *away* from the future. Or why
taking cashmere out of the washer is like plunging
one's hands into warm pudding. How one goes from India
to Jell-O so fast! Turquoise to mosquito. Where does the cold go?
Once-shivering children now parade like Roman aristocrats
round the pool. They don't care that northern France melts
from right to left, or hear the sparrows sing *ouvrir*.
They don't see daylilies beg for alms, or the ocean bow
in prayer, quartz and feldspar smithereened on the shore.
                    There is a unit of time, named Eclipse Season,
lasting 173.31 days. There is a cumulus cloud, not caught
in your window, scudding along the bowl of sky. Yes, of course
there is a face, darkening, brightening. There are many faces
bathed briefly in the blues and yellows, reds and greens, and death

comes for them all. When it comes for me, I think I will be
sleeping, birds and mice making small noises in the dark.
One lamp will have been left on at a window. And someone
I care for will be holding my hand, but it will not be you.
I will die knowing less than I know now: That I bartered
my children for words and my words for love. That all my debts
were paid in full. And that when I was finally a child again myself,
scared, hungry, and cold, I was aware of none of this.
And it was then I found a mother in the world I'd been born into
long ago. Together we made one wing, one leaf, our veins like theirs
in sun or moon, and so beautiful I can close my eyes and still see.

WORD PROBLEM WITH WAVES IN ITS HAIR

There were 20 frittatas in that oven at any given time
They were little frittatas
There were starlings nesting in the wall beside the fridge
The knob on the oven looked like the combination lock to a safe
I desired to turn it in my hand like a curl in my mother's hair
She took me to the beach when she wanted waves in mine
She wanted to put some body in it she said
She already had my brother in her
He was a guppy in her belly then & I her starfish all replaceable appendage
Shells thrilled me always filled with something brains or flakes off the moon
And jellyfish like the inside of an elbow
My mother liked her beach stones wet & her sand dry
A flash mob of Zsa Zsas on the busy lip of every cresting wave
But nothing not even the sun could make me squint like the sharp tips of her
glistening hair
The octopus has 8 arms she said 3 hearts
Octo 8 Carry the 3
Plus there are 2 sides to each horizon as there are to every wall
There were never frittatas in that oven
But she may have mentioned them once
When long straw & short straw were the verticals we made
Our different hair whipping greetings
Though our backs were to them all

PERPENDICULAR

It would have been a fine path for a lizard to cross
but I saw none. Brambles and sweetbriar grew
on the town side, poppies and wild grasses on the river.
Too hot for birds, the ducks were out, in water and mud,
and frogs were out, by the hundreds it seemed, saying,
Way, Way, in their deepest voices. It was beautiful there
but I'd seen beauty and its opposite so often
that when warmth broke over my skin I remembered winter,
the way fresh grief undoes you the moment you're fully awake.
I asked my young friend, when she turned two,
what she would serve at her birthday party and she said,
Tofu and cupcakes. When she was three and I was very sad
she called and said, What are you doing? Picking flowers?
She talked in poems like she was dreaming all the time
or very old or Virginia Woolf. More often in the "first" world
one wakes *from* not *to* the nightmare. When I dreamed I lost
my love I willed myself awake because I would not
survive the pain again, even dreaming. Which is responsible
for that mercy, Doktor, the conscious or the un-? I want
the poppies picked and I want the poppies left where they grow.
Like looking through the window of a moving train
at someone walking up a road lined with poplars
and being someone walking up a road lined with poplars.
The train and the trees, a shower of petals and bees,
sun on the glass and the train perpendicular to the road.
Things entirely themselves arriving in the deep
double shadows of the grass and passersby.

FEBRUARY AND AUGUST

August brought its usual stalks, then dust, then gold.
It brought its own dry voice that said, I have things
I want to tell you but I should say I love you first.

In my color wheel, always slow to turn, the field had stayed
February, stubbled with ice, summer below like the rooms of Augustus,
the piss and blood wall paints expertly preserved.

To prevent overwatering, place two ice cubes in your orchid
once a week. I put them in the blossoms and they kept falling out.
The importance of clarity cannot be overstated.
Or is it charity we cherish most? This time it would be

cello-deep, train at the ear and core-heat clear. This time
would be geology not archaeology, summer as cisseason.
Emperor Mammatus offering the only coffered ceiling.
Then fox, then sunset, then other rampant strata from the dig.

WIDOWS AND BRIDES

Professoressa Panella released a statement to the Italian press:
We have unearthed more than ten rooms, beautiful mosaic
floors and frescoed walls. Without photos, I am forced to imagine
her eyeliner, glossy as starlings, as strains of Noh
on vinyl drift over the Palatine.

Domus Augusti. Livia's rooms. But what of *these* rooms,
with their smell of feet and crush of complex dresses,
live voices inside them like pockets of snow:

Will you take a picture for my mother? Imagine me
ten pounds lighter. Do you prefer the empire
waist or the sleeveless?
                                    I like best the button at the wrist,
though impractical in summer, I know. O do come back
soon, Toklas wrote, years after Stein's death, I shan't last forever.

TACTILE SYCAMORE

Up close, bark cracks, curls, and peels on the sun-
facing sides. Everywhere else is tight, black, and lichen.
                    /
When I pick up the pieces,
they close round the heat of my hand like a hand.
                    /
Sycamore, you, too, pulled the wool over my eyes. From afar,
light as butter cream in a green dish.
                    /
Once, she brought me breath in her gloved hands;
my hair, a viral resistance among her fingers.
                    /
Sycamore. Sick amour. Seek no more. Skip to
my lou. My skin. My bark. My blight is
not worse than my   /

SELF-PORTRAIT AS SYCAMORE IN COPPER & PEARL

I may look smooth-
        shouldered just stepping
                from the soak, my planes
                        flushed pink, angles
ocher, my tresses
        oxidizing in reverse,
                but take a long hard
                        look. Take a biopsy.
Interrogate my juices
        under your scope &
                you'll survive as I have
                        the sylvan hallelujah
moments, bullion bars
        fanning through the showy
                oaks & maples & the sweet
                        sweet gums. When blue is
dominant all over
        the earth, atmosphere is king,
                the air so hammers-on-
                        strings-perfect it steals
the voices right off
        the birds. In the double Dutch
                sunlight of American mid-October,
                        therefore, I may look like
a pearl, but try stopping one,
        its cheeks packed with
                gold, silver & blood.
                        Observe its divots
& dents. Likewise, I
        am flawed, with flaking

                    crusts, molds, blighted bits,
                                    & not a few limbs dead
as a gelding's part.
                    I know the need to admire
                            one's cream blushes & metallic
                                    finishes, to take a copper
leaf for your collection
                    & break the ricochet
                            silence en plein air with your
                                    sighs. But understand, rainlight
is the truest pearl, and
                    my ugliest friend,
                            with whom I have neither
                                    inhibitions nor differences.

CHORAL SYCAMORES: A VALEDICTION

the heart still beating / Under the bark
—OVID

The day-moon halved and see-through in the sky
Might make it hard enough for you to mind
Your feet.
        But then there's us, our bones on blue,
Our panicked manes, snow flurries fixed or lightning's
Ragged wedding swatches hung.
                You know
The bow that frosts the cello's strings? We're after
That. That blizzard in the brain, electric
Synapses alight and cracking knuckles
In the belljar.
        The side the sun finds finds
Us flare. The side sun can't, a timber-rotted
Mud, the negative of us, our postures
No less carved by wind for that, our scribbled
Tips aloft, air trash in the subway, frenzy
Of Daphne's upraised hands and hair.
              Like her
We are beheld unheld; we will not leave
The earth alive.
        Nor will you, in your scuffed shoes—
Our hollows, too, large enough to hide the horses in.

INSCRIPTION

Canal du Midi, France

Arcades of plane trees arc *AVE*s above the canal.
I know they are not a choir.
I know they are not Kabuki, tusk, knuckle, or
the swords and flames Saint Joan rode into,
though it's true I think of them as these,
and as the sky's deep pockets of snow, white keys,
mammoth teeth. It is my way and my need:
mes amours, sycamores. My emblems on a crest,
gallery of visible ghosts. Mostly I love the light
they hold inside, the all-too-much and aged *toujours*
of them, their airborne electricities. Who's to explain
affinities like these? Two seas were joined this way
in 1681, sparing sailors from piracy and storms.
In the 1830s, planes were planted on its banks
to protect vacationers from sun. Now a careless
tourist nicks a tree with rope and spreads disease
that will kill them all. *Ceratocystis platani,* traced
to munitions boxes brought by World War II GIs.
42,000 must be felled and burned to save, scientists
hope, the remaining planes, cousin to our sycamore,
that is the wood that made the box that held
the fungus riding in the waters of the canal.
Measures have been taken. The road to hell, etc.
Saint Joan, finally, was burned to death for the cross-
dressing; Kabuki theaters incinerated by soldiers
for their drag shows and wartime sympathies.
Sorrow. Desire. There are so many auto fatalities
on plane-lined streets here, the French joke

about why the tree crossed the road. They burn
the hollows out sometimes. Inscribe vaginal lips
around the gashes in swaths of hot pink paint.
What we leave behind and what is left of us
are related questions. The graves in town are up
to three centuries old. Some crypts, forged crosses,
chipped wreaths of ceramic flowers. Earth gouged,
trees felled, buildings razed, never mind the lives.
In the New World, a fungus-resistant sycamore
is bred to replace relatives destroyed at the canal.
Measures taken. Like swapping out the burnt-out
bulbs on a string of Christmas lights. So what
if we are replaceable? Mostly I love how
we burst the prisons of our skins and shine.
Outside the cemetery, someone's Magic-Markered
a locked electrical box with the words *Sexe Toyes*.
The plaques on the graves nearby are inscribed
Souvenirs and *Regrets*. Which are, even in my language,
polite ways of saying *Done*.

ELEVEN-SIDED POEM

after Carlos Drummond de Andrade's "Seven-Sided Poem"

When I was dead, one of the whiter
sycamores who live on the river said,
Kathy, why didn't you live in your body more?

To which the oak added, That's not an accusation;
that's a sympathetic question.

Little sumac said, Don't step on me, even in your spectral form!
The beech asked, Could we be cousins?
And the fig, Why did you never properly learn
to braid your hair?

When sequoia called to say,
You broke your vows, the birches said,
Take us with you; the birds went with her.

Magnolia, redbud, and cottonwood said,
Our hearts bleed, the way the rain.
But willow could say only, Garland, Tinsel.
As if I alone had been responsible for Christmas.

So I said, Listen, you trees
(though I could not speak),
I remember dying
to grow up. Standing
on tiptoe to pull my own baby
teeth. Crushing my pelvis
to kill any unborn hunched

in the warm center. I sometimes stayed
there myself. I sometimes left
for a long time and was late to return.

But I learned again, knees small and high, teeth
showing when I smiled,
clock after clock until quarter after clock,
sugar everywhere, loose and in cubes.
Açúcar it's called, where I was conceived.

A man came round with his paint
roller to re-frost the scuffed bits.
(Men are whitewashing both sides of the equator.)
Someone brought his bird to the pool,
arranged a chaise for each of them.
Mothers with children in water wings.

I stepped into water as warm as my body was before I forgot it.
And the cold air after—
I had forgotten that, too.

Oh, but the meringue of the clouds was sweet
that second time. Copious
reasons for squinting, skin
wet or dry, one large hand untangling my hair.

You trees, I assure you, I was in full
possession of my body when I died,
all four of our blue eyes licked
and all the candles blown.

NOTES

The John Berryman epigraph is a remix of lines from "Dream Song 1."

"*Caro Nome*" is for Mio. We miss you.

Elelendish is an archaic word meaning "foreign."

"How We Looked" is for Pablo Tanguay.

"The Signal Master's Song" is for Philip Grandinetti.

"Perpendicular" is for Marlene Kocan.

ACKNOWLEDGMENTS

I am deeply grateful to Daniel Slager and the Milkweed staff, to Wayne Miller, Martha Collins, and Christopher Howell. I am indebted to the editors and readers who helped me get these poems out into the world, especially at a time when publishing seemed only for the strong: John Gallaher, David Young, Mike Madonick, Lisa Lewis, Mark Bibbins, Erin Belieu, and Natalie Shapero. Loving thanks and farewell to my teachers Ben Jameson, Mark Strand, and Philip Levine. Finally, I thank with all my heart those who kept me warm through winter, and Philip, who brought me summer.

* * *

Grateful acknowledgment is made to the editors of the following literary journals and online venues where many of these poems were published, sometimes in different forms: the Academy of American Poets *Poem-A-Day* series ("Snow Globe"), The Awl ("Sycamores at High Noon," "Sycamore in the Weak Light of Early Spring," "Choral Sycamores: A Valediction," and "Word Problem with Waves in Its Hair"), *Birmingham Poetry Review* ("Sycamore Envies the Cottonwoods behind Your Place"), *Cimarron Review* ("Black Walnuts" and "Shoo Fly"), *Connotations Press/ Congeries* ("Elelendish," "Poem with Its Heart Buried under the Floorboards" and "Life, with Eyeliner"), *Diode* ("Split" and "Waiting Area Atrium"), *FIELD* ("Letter to What's Mostly Missing" and "The White, the Red & the Pink In-Between"), *Fogged Clarity* ("Sycamore in Jericho"), *Harlequin* ("February and August"), *Hazlitt* ("Middle-Aged Sycamore"), *Kenyon Review* ("Structural Engineering" and "Widows and Brides"), *Laurel Review* ("Cinder" and "The Signal Master's Song"), *Miramar* ("Nervure" and "Eleven-Sided Poem"), *New Republic* ("No Meteor"), *Ninth Letter* ("Suburban Canticle," "Ode to Julia Morgan," and "Sycamore, Wick & Flame"), *Ocean State Review* ("Convent of Santa Chiara and the Poor Clares"), *One* ("Ruin"), *Poetry* ("*Caro Nome*," "Perpendicular," and "Inscription"), *This Land Press: Poetry to the People* ("Kaboom Pantoum"), *Willow Springs* ("Self-Portrait as Sycamore in Copper and Pearl"), *Zone 3* ("How We Looked"). "Shoo Fly" also appeared on *Verse Daily*.

Fritha Strand

KATHY FAGAN is the author of four previous collections, including the National Poetry Series selection *The Raft* and Vassar Miller Prize winner *MOVING & ST RAGE*. Her work has appeared in the *Paris Review, Kenyon Review, Slate, Field, Poetry, New Republic,* and *Missouri Review,* among other literary magazines. She teaches at Ohio State University, where she is also the poetry editor of OSU Press, and advisor to *The Journal.* She lives in Columbus, Ohio.

Founded as a nonprofit organization in 1980, Milkweed Editions is an independent publisher. Our mission is to identify, nurture and publish transformative literature, and build an engaged community around it.

milkweed.org

Interior design by Mary Austin Speaker
Typeset in Adobe Caslon

A long-running serif font first designed by William Caslon in 1722, Adobe Caslon was used widely in the early days of the American colonies. Adobe Caslon was used for the US Declaration of Independence, but fell out of use soon after the Revolutionary War. It has been revived at various times, notably during the British Arts and Crafts movement.

Printed in the USA
CPSIA information can be obtained
at www.ICGtesting.com
JSHW080005150824
68134JS00021B/2293

9 781571 314734